WHEN A GIRL LOVES A GIRL

JEREMY REED is the author of over fifty books of award-winning poetry, fiction and biography, and also a celebrated performer of his work with Itchy Ear as The Ginger Light. Concerned with writing from the visionary present into the near future, J. G. Ballard described Reed's talent as "almost extraterrestrial in its brilliance." Controversial, edge-walking and propelled by luminous imagination, he has for both his work and looks been described as "British poetry's glam, spangly, shape-shifting answer to David Bowie." Amongst his recent books are the poetry collections *Sooner or Later Frank*, *Candy4Cannibals* and *Psychedelic Meadow*, and two non-fiction books, *The Dilly: A Secret History of Piccadilly Rent Boys*, and a biography of Lou Reed titled *Waiting for the Man*. He lives in London.

JEREMY REED

WHEN A GIRL LOVES A GIRL

SAPPHO REMADE

THIS IS A SNUGGLY BOOK

Copyright © 2020

by Jeremy Reed.

All rights reserved.

ISBN: 978-1-64525-022-7

for Carmen Montenegro

WHEN A GIRL LOVES A GIRL

1

That beach-babe, she goes unchanged year by year,
a sort of sunshine mirage, don't abate
my interest in her vampy sexiness
and like a pop song she will break my heart:

just come down out of the sky as avatar,
a shimmer in sea fog, I need her now
of all times leave her father's golden house
sometimes she's Martine or Aphrodita

a need to share her as transcendent glow
arrived on black earth like a re-entry
demanding why, yet generous again
with fuck-ups in my scandalous love-life

associatively linked to poetry
I note the black quartz grains dusting her toes,
her quizzical surprise 'you called me down
and now I'm here as time-slipped intermediary'

a tantalising give and take away
perversely self-deflected empathy
girl on the run also wanting to stay
and being both incites renewed desire

to win her love—'Sappho you shape my name
like someone standing on the horizon
throwing a call, come on babe, get it on;'
her footprints scattered across nude gold beach.

2

Yellowing apple trees
some ritual site under
sweet smoke of libanum
drizzling incentive
too spooky to go near

It's the percussive crash of two apples
cheek to cheek thud
in rolling ricochet, clash.
The water's cold as chilled vodka,
big roses drop pouty shadows,
when the light fades leaves shiver
flipped over by lazy breeze.

Horses wade through flowers
snuffling deep grass
with clouds swimming on their backs.
We'll beat out a rhythm
on drumskins and wine
combine and kinda
dance

3

What's unforgettable and never leaves my mind
the beauty of each summer's tangy girls
incisive strap-marks like white geometry

4

I loved you Atthis future tourist
arrived too early or too late, don't know

5

These same-sex girls, wrists fluent as roses,
heads full of dope and smoke's their greenish cloud
they visit me stoned dopamine sisters
as psychoactive gold on gold on gold

6

When you're processed into death, as remains,
your name wiped into anonymity.
you'll be recognised in the underworld
as having refused Pieria's roses,
and loiter in Aida's black marble hall,
knowing that losers only lose again
and there's no bottom line to losing out.

7

Dika, improvise with your stem-thin wrists
flower designs to accessorise built blonde hair
for those anxious with slaved portfolios
arrest you as activist, shame you out

8

Spring as slow emergent expectancy—
Gongyla (never heard that name before)

and has the avatar posted a sign
to my girl gang that Hermes slipped
into my dream as transgender

or bad news him being around
in the wrong band
impending some finality

except for those who long to die
and see the druggy lotus on black ponds
of marshy Acheron

9

I've got distracted structuring a dress,
love on my mind, don't blame me babe
split between a cute boy and a zingy girl

10

Is it a pop song that has me dream again
of a blue beachworld in my miraged teens?

11

Sit under trees, a summer festival
the girls place leaf-crowns in their hair

12

I fall asleep on her cleavage
and smell the sun bloc filming her nipples

13

On a rainy day's torrential dazzle
one blue teardrop-shaped raindrop, a god's eye

14

Crying ASIA and sweated-out
the runner emerges from gritty dust
like a man materialised out of a cloud
shouting EKTOR like a mantra
hear me loud, EKTOR EKTOR

They bring a black-eyed sex-slave
from Bangkok (suits the name)
an import with a boatload
of curvy Asian teens.
There's gold chains, purple coats,
bashed silverware, ivory,
a heap of toys manufactured in Taiwan.

The dehydrated runner
gets bottled water and the city out
for a spontaneous festival
marshalls mounted on steaming black horses
navigate a trancy compliant crowd

singing its way up from the sea
beating a tight bongo on skins
stoned on a brew offered in bowls,
cassia, olibanum, myrrh, psilocybin.
It's Ektor and Andromeda
they'll celebrate as married on the beach
like a delusional holo in gold haze
mistaken as the day of forever.

15

I'm all shook up, the need for sex
surging through me like roaring wind at night
flipping over the undersides of leaves

16

Your shyness worked on me ingénue
centuries before Lolita made a name
like strawberry ice cream topping

17

Who's the wild girl in that hand-me-down frock
(no taste) got you under her spell
don't know nothing but country dialect
she's let her hem ride high
that better sits at her burnished anklet

18

With eyes that aqueous marine green
they get back what they see equalised
perfect dissolve between seer and seen

19

Itinerant swallow, why me
who intersects with your moment in time
when we don't share the same reality

20

That man leaning in on you changes skin
into mutant, like he's a Bowie-type,
a blond smile, sexually ambiguous

he sips at soft inflexions in his voice,
fields liquid laughter, invites slow revenge
I'm up for with instantaneous hate.

My tongue turns dry as a nervy lizard,
fire seethes like poison in my arteries
blood roars like the underground in my ears,

then the cold shakes set in, I'm eaten up
dead or alive, I know only the space
in which I'm neither focused nor on attack

21

A bolt out of the flaming peacock sky
nude Eros in a Phoenician red shirt
arrives so fast he never started out

22

The word messaged, Andromeda was shoved
from every summer rite and festival:
Sappho was in, I run into myself

unlocking atoms for the company.
Chanced on a hottie in Kypros
blue sunshine irised in her eyes
like psychedelics, can't grow old

or be sucked into oozy Acheron.

23

I never got lucky at dressmaking
this other girl got crowned with golden leaves
and didn't even chip black nail polish

24

Gongyla, sing to us on the rainy beach,
she's back again the blonde in pleated skirt
the one idealised in stormy blues

you don't get over, always out of reach

25

Armed police and urban terrorists
don't do it for me, nor orbital ships.
But you Elena, left your man for me
and now I sit on islands in your eyes.

26

I

She shipped to Troy, disowned her ID,
just cleared out led astray by me—
a suitcase of black dresses and a gun
and Anaktoria now gone away

got closer to her than her skin:
and now I watch her walk multiple curves
like she's treading on oranges
rolling away under her feet

II

And Helen, like a blonde Russian reward
liberated same-sex, you couldn't tell
her hair from sunshine, walked out on the lot

into her myth, and just became a name,
the archetype you search for on beaches.
Men set fire to themselves looking for her

self-cremated in thick coils of black smoke

Remember me ANAKTORIA TORIA
I'd even kiss your echo like sea-fog

CODA

They cooked up psychoactives, poppy heads
fermented, and drank off the juice
to see the gods come down from the mountain
led by Leonard Cohen
and shared it as a firelit collective
exchanging bodies like the gift of rings

27

Suddenly this invasion of the shore
marguerites with their golden fried-egg eyes

28

Gorgo's too much, comes on at me all night
With poems written underneath her feet

29

An ivory clasp that's what she left behind
a used boarding pass and a memory
circulating like Chanel No 5

30

They wear scarlet bandanas in their hair,
our girl gang, youth makes summer twice as long
listening to the right hooky song

I remember your bunchy yellow curls
got lost in them, patted their gloss,
our head scarves mostly embroidered Persian,

and Kleis I'll get the one you really want
given the chance. That was our summer look,
our names dispersed, each generation thinks

for a summer that it's the first and last

31

Her tiny feet are like a footbinder's
an estimated shoe-size 2

32

Go marry someone half your age
it's me your lover tells you this,
the older one, skinned by the bathroom mirror
into forensic self-appraisal

33

Late evening dazzle, smoggy western star
occluded light like orange juice,
your daughter she's a runaway
can't take it anymore out on the road
honey, she's going far

34

That boy you've got, he's cute,
ambiguously sexed
in gay bars and out
thinner than a carnation stem
knowing he rules the summer from his hips

35

Cytherean priestess
the one who hijacked my identity
in a weird symbiotic way
has chased off into the forest
as green energies

36

Irana, with you I can't concentrate
on anything but being without YOU

37

She's like the nuttiest tasting apple
bursting with sweetness highest on the tree,
the one elusively just out of reach
the focal curve a glossy two-tone shine.

Everywhere saturated hyacinths
the mountain purple with indigo glow

38

Ermonia, you can't source her data
she's platinum as Elena's bleached bob,
and gets me hot to correct her suave posh
overdone formality, kick her in

the river dazzling outside the window
and how to make it last all night

39

It's down to us to remember Sardis
the way she danced, sexual autonomy
in every ripple and back of the night
a red moon, like you'd park a car on it

that close up, post-apocalyptic red.
She led us into country, meadows rinsed
with purple clover, a rose in her hair
and Atthis was the girl got into her
body and soul: they sang the song.
They left us without compass in drenched fields
of popping dew, our only recourse wine,
a white that hit me from my head to toes

neon red lunar eclipse, late July,
my lack of lovers desperate, I sing

they come and go

40

Her shoes were Camper, scarlet soles
Asian toes lacquered navy with white bands

41

Mika, you've gone poured petrol on my heart
by taking Penthilea from my bed.
I can't stand up to your duplicity—
her Chanel cloud still throws its force around,
I sing my loss as abject poetry
that doesn't heal me, just joins up the lines.

42

Mischief or bad lack, something in between
excites like lightning scattering

43

Up on the centre stage and from Lesbos
he holds his own as audience
the poet reading in a thunderstorm

44

Her father's Kronos, sounds like Russian beer
her tits are violet romanced areolas

45

In Crete we danced together only girls
in a collective: it was proto-gay
our circle reaching into each other
like locking a beaded necklace

46

Same-sex Arkheanassa and Gorgo
sleep together in a red king-sized bed
one body fits two in sexy design
like a banana and its skin.
Gongyla and Gorgo, they're tongue on tongue
as a rogue body, and sometimes they're meshed
like a new slippery species making out.

47

A dream-consultancy, I talked to him
whatever shape lived on that blue island
instructively, like talking to myself
through somebody else's voice

48

Those luscious pleasures with Andromeda
(why don't I rhyme her name with mascara)
persist like rippling waves running for shore

49

That blonde, she's richest yellow-gold,
can't tell her from a flower, sumptuous iris
on the pouty folds of a brimming rose,
a look that shivers on the edge of dilution
into impossible beauty, wouldn't exchange
her for a hundred Mytilenean virgins

50

Times I'm solo, no one in my life no
sitting in a moody harbour bar,
turquoise shimmer, re-evaluate
how her snug body fitted mine
better than Gyrinno's more like a boy's

51

I'd have a rose break into speech
for beauty's secret, crimson lexicon
like opening petals of her twirly clitoris

52

Brightness, vivacity has me climb out
black mood
and sight a ship destabilised off-coast
shoving at
waves like a tractor

Nothing to do but keep a glow
for its safe passage, a black ship
bulked with cargo roughed up by white weather

you ever seen a white rainbow?

53

Aphrodita, all those peachy vowels
condensed into a name, sits by hemmed waves—
a virtual substantiated by a pill

54

A purple silk bandana, it's her look
at festivals, gifted by Phokaia
listening to bands amped up in pastoral

55

She's got no equal, cuts it in her style,
my lover's mismatched turquoise and green eyes

56

Percussive vibration in every cell
the beat of SEX, I'm thrown again
by libidinous hold
making me shiver, need it now
sweat and honey, this coming on
in spasms, chemicals that hit the sky

57

Your hate's like bitter chocolate turning sweet
Atthis, I bought you a new white shirt-dress
but still you pile drinks on Andromeda

58

You'll never be back now the rain's set in
Pollyana, Polyanaktidas, you're history
gone like skimmed eye-contact in the subway crowd

59

Golden goblets to use on golden sands
brimming with sunsets active in the wine

60

I'm bound to Aphrodita, a sex-slave
tighter than black skin to a grape

61

Poetry's my obsession for the few
it travels like red wavelengths from the sun
maybe outlives me, don't do me no good
remembered in another century

62

Collapsed in tears like rain on a window
trouble banging around in the kitchen
I got beaten with bruises like black plums

63

Hanging around again for the right girl
always the imaginary one I lost

64

Can't see the stars in daylight for the sun
Venus looks brighter for the full-on moon

65

Diamond and gold fillings for kleptocrats,
billionaire kings, they don't notice poets
gold in their veins as lyric currency

66

Why don't you leave off her violet nipples?
We'll interfere with songs outside your door
in deep night, chant to interrupt excess.

Call up your single friends to bike over
on oily Hondas: we'll sing to the stars.
It's only girls collect protectively.

It's one of ours you've got, so we maintain
strict vigilance, she's softer than the thought
of soft compatible with a pink rose.

Just leave her be, go back to biker friends,
we'll stay a menace posted round the house
kicking up noise like a girl garage band

67

It started young this itch called poetry
like I tickled my voice with a feather
and it was never far from me
the word as transcendent unit

Now we walk to a wedding
on the road to the gold mountain
where nine strippers sing

68

Those closest to my heart most hurt
bring me to my knees in the shower
digging at scratches in the aqua tiles

69

Loving you I longed to die
rather than lose. You rolled over:
terror like thunder gripped me on the bed.
Your tears were gin-clear as you pulled away

telling me we were through, no coming back.
You told me like they always do
remember good times, like the flowers she wove
into my hair so optimally,

the way we oiled each other as one skin,
luxuriated on red silk cushions,
painted each other's toes, blue, green, black, red,
all those caked bottles dried out on the shelf

70

First news of springtime it's the hyacinth's
frizzy uncoiling purple perm

71

I lack gold honey engineered by bees
buy Manuka as alchemical resource

72

Let Kyprian wallop you with reproach,
bitterer, loud-mouthed at finding you out
Dorikha, love-bites pitted on your skin
from someone finished you a second time

73

Around you Atthis steam clouds in the shower
repeated like palaces in the sky

74

Dorikha ah ah called you half-asleep
her coldness scrutinising your choc moles
Dorikha ah ah what does she want of you

75

Your skincare's bright green gel, Japan import
I smeared it too, the association
a fetish, clearer on your face than light

76

Burnt offering, a personal ritual
drizzled in smoke, you left your shoes behind
come back again from the mountain

77

Help comes to hand; whatever's feminine
inspires—I write poems under your feet
micro haiku that I read out to you

78

What's it you grieve, a beautiful body
I gave you and turned out no good
in Starbucks, you ambivalent

still hung up on the basest man
no clue to you, that little trace of Joy
by Jean Patou might bring you luck

79

Perfect, a monumental single rose
bleeding red petals to dissolution

80

I'll be remembered but never know it
a posthumous mirage
picked up in Foyles
bitty fragments like crisps

81

Bad money, cryptocurrencies, they rot
like Alzheimer's where there's no poetry.
Build lyric into cloud, you get it right
as riches raining down on the city

82

Sometimes I tell myself that her closed eyes
get recharged greener when she sleeps

83

It's more melodious than the harp
listening to gold atoms vibrate in light

84

Auriferous dawn like a red tulip
expanding right across the hemisphere

85

You came back home wasted from Negronis
your tongue vicious from thunder in the mix

86

You wear your figure outside a silk dress
its ivory contours a skin dissolve
for you beauty's the seamless fit

87

Our moment maxxed on pleasure, all my girls
at a beach party, there's no song
retrieves it, just the halo of a glow

88

These macho guys all of a type
not even bi dupe girls into their way
of treating emotions like real estate

89

There's one moment stands out in every life
the witness remakes a shared thing
like who can tell the diamond from the light

90

Love's so incredible it turns to myth
it's bittersweet like black chocolate
and a viral carrier of twisted pain

100

I

I make her CUM Polyanaktidas
(six syllable name like a position)
using a dildo, it's like playing chords
    to hear her sing
as clitoral tango the way we do
each other, mysteries, orgies
    they're both the same
in the goldrush of orgasm
Polyanaktidasit's in the name
kicking the sheets to a satin whirlpool

II

Her man's demoralised
as if I care
won't take it girl on girl

and Poly's my cousin
skin to skin
he's left out in the cold
can't stop our lubricious tempo
O O O

101

He walks like Ares, call him Harry
on his marriage night, he's 6' 7"
like another tower on the skyline
the sort of man you dream grows in the ground
vertically taller than a sunflower

102

Those islanders dusted by Kypros sand
help me get my runaway brother back
who clean disappeared, got to smuggling drugs—
he's out there like a halo in the fog
and I'll forgive most anything, love him
as history shared, I'm waiting on the beach
for drop-off from a boat, don't see a thing
their balaclavas like a panda's face

Let's get him clean, dress him in a white shirt,
have him raise his arms up to the sun

103

They're praying, the princes of Atreos,
forgotten cult, all those dead kings
gone back into the sun.

Thyona's returned, stepped out of a flower,
perfect girlfriend for the right girl
doing the rounds as one on one

104

I

Part illusion, part freak autonomy
it's Hera shows up in my consciousness
sudden the way those Mycenaean kings
as kleptocratic autocrats

collapsed when tanks rolled into Troy
turned homeward down the racing Skamander
luckless royals hauling suitcases of cash
pursued by border police across frontiers

discredited: I too need sanctuary—
a yard in which to dance and build my songs
like mantra, all those molecules of breath
in utterance atomised into gold

II

Epochs get deleted by history:
Atridaean princes, whose heard of them
pissing out losses up against a wall

and exiled in a huddle of black cars?
I too need asylum, hold up my hand
As though I'll catch an answer from the sky.

105

What's your summer compass in sapphire heat
Kypros; Paphos or Panormos
blue on blue on blue on blue

106

You make me hot, even my nude body's
a barrier to sex I want

107

Wasted by the excesses of the night
we find our clothes again, get up, get out,
there's issues clearer for bright light

108

You've been and gone, my red desire
that burnt me up is quietened now
but only like an interval of storm

109

Even your dress size goes from 10 to 12
but beauty's compacted to a gold fit.

110

I'm panicked, confused, all beat up inside,
even the floor keeps orbiting my mind

111

He got her in the end, the first and last,
the only one, intuitive magic
as initiative, fitted each other
like wine a glass, you see it in her face
serene surprise at overtakenness

112

She wears a red dress with a yellow top
you'd question the co-ordinates
her eyes first time are blue and second green
debating on a Phyrigian red carpet
why inspiration lifts her off her feet

113

Dawn, and I paint my toenails gold
at the exact moment hoping I'll fly

114

Can't get it back evanescent girlhood
teen wonder and its hormonal exhaust
up all night partying, she'll never now
share what I remember I've lost
vivacity like slicing a lemon

115

Virulent black dreams scaring up
psychic shattering, autonomous grief
tearing me up in streaming rites
no sleeping drug disqualifies
I'm so broke up and in my dream
fell from a tower into drop
got woken and the residue's
a grainy start

116

They don't come twice like her the one
I picked up for our mental symmetry
the way she is, those cool blue beads

popping with stormy heartbeats at her throat

117

That guy's circle of friends is used beer cans
he's up to marry and they're all the same
the idea of the girl's not her at all

better go juice a bike into the hills

118

Pleasure's a way of damping grief
like Valium.
The day after tomorrow's how it feels

this fusion of the two like gin and lime,
peeling the bandaging, go on and hurt,
love's like self-harm, always the deepest cut

119

Clear clean song tremulous as Neil Young
floating a lyric in blue mountain air

120

Brightness so iridescent in her eyes
each brain cell's a molecular diamond

121

Under the full moon they stood in a ring
teleporting to its grey regolith
a psychedelic the carrier

122

To Gyrinno they'll wonder who you were
back from the future as a single word

123

I'll put a purple cushion under you
your blouse off, then your bra, see what we make

of nipples licked to magenta alert
like two rain-popped magnolias

124

Pieria, I found the muses there
nine of them in a café face-spotting
for someone to inspire with poetry

125

They're topless on the beaches in my cove
violet tits let them chase the blues away
conical rewards for my dancing eyes

126

My inspirers have luxurious blonde hair
falls like a silk torrent on what I write

127

He's dying Kytherea, up in the hills,
this kid you'd think a god for looks
of Aids on a silk cushioned bed—

Adonis, thin as spiky light,
and what to do, demand intervention
I ripped my dress up and it did no good
wailing there in shreds

127

All and the other, that's the chosen one
retouching China-red lipstick in a bar

128

The poem, it's more valuable than gold
vowels as its carats never loses shine

129

I trace your gold scent Chanel No 5
as sexy pheromones, olfactory swirl
like a scent halolasy
I'll be by

130

Those discords, disruptively dissonant
won't climb into the smoky sky
like a guitar massaged into screaming feedback

131

Seven directions in terror seven
    the laurel tree's the inspirer
not density of pine
    a hut in the empty

insidious leaf-rufflings of a mouse.
Wanna go through green shade with you

Your girlish heart, kiss you under laurel
    seven I associate
with you
    times I found your beauty out

132

Artemis what I SEE IN YOU
is looks that break me up indescribably
at mystery of your chemistry

133

You too, Kalliopa, you wear your skin
outside your dress, leave me in a daze

134

I called you (new phone) late in life
later than I'd admit, voice full of girls,
those names like open petals
end in an A.
I'd dyed my hair blacker (obsidian)
lost dexterity, still the dawn
opened a red auroral rose in me
and I've got prospects with a girl
I'll wear in me like a snake-ring
and round my body like a curve.
A last lover, no a new shine
as continuity, like she's the sun
explicitly gold-red at my window
the glow starting again

135

I'm willing: that means popping boundaries
like living tomorrow before today

136

You know the story, Leda found a purple egg,
took a snapshot, titled it *Alien*

137

Softer than a rose, your red oval mouth
Before the lipstick bleeds

138

Dying's so retrograde to what we build
as personal. Don't happen to the gods
whose genes are indestructible

139

Fucking's the way to earn longevity.
I wish it on you two
the prospective goldrush of orgasm.

140

Massaged harp surprises on a mountain
Maria-Christina plays a blue rainbow

141

My list of loves they're in my head
and walk back through me like a corridor

142

I'm childless, same-sex addicted,
don't know if that's fulfilment, but a need
in living free from that man thing
that don't improve, demand
command I'd rather be without
same love's voluptuous
like two bodies fitting one dress

143

It's sung elegy cleans the house
after a death, the nine muses lived here
leaving behind eighteen gold strappy sandals
to be worn to reach the heights

144

Return inspirers, re-commit magic
to elevating every gold syllable

145

The festival this year they've got the Stones
stoking aviation noise, riff-thunder
as stratospheric rumble, heard it yet—
'Gimme Shelter' boiling right up the spine

146

Eros, child of Gea and Ouranos
split like a dahlia into red and white

147

She ran away a teen to a brothel
coercive daughter of Aphrodita
learnt persuasion by glossing her toes red

148

Medea, I left you as a single name
no details added to my phone

149

Lato and Nioba fumed in my time
as lovers didn't need a man between
the chocolate and its pink wrapper

150

Polychromatic effulgence colours
like psychedelics enhancing vision

151

Poets give and never receive
proportionate to generosity,
so, he said
who was he

152

Me gone my own way
friction Andromeda
slamming doors warring
girls against girls
like domestic thunder

Tyndarides messed it up
those mansion blocks and palaces
in which we stayed on and off
now guarded by security

tough doorman
with a grudge against gay
like a buzz-cut psycho

153

Night turns my eyes black, blacker sleep
completes dissolve into obsidian

154

I'm yours, the word darling
sounds like putting on a ring

155

That couple, same-sex marriage on the beach exchange pink roses, eat the lotus flower

156

Of the Muses, they're lightning in the nerves
their dance point is each syllable
their signature rolls away like thunder

157

The island Aiga it's a blue mirage
like a UFO sighting off Samoa
shaped like a popcorn nugget in the strait

158

Barbitos, Baromos, Barmos
a triumvirate of beach villa gays
mixed negronis, believed they'd outlive time

159

Flick of tissue round an orange stick
dipped in peroxide and wiped under nails

160

The dress: an imported black Shangtung sheath
moulded to me like a liquid contour

161

Here again tomorrow before today
time's like an imaginary movie

162

She calls her daughter while she's in my bed
like it's a threesome that we're missing out

163

She picks the opened flower, eye to eye
exchanging its identity with hers

164

Remember in our teens deserted me
hot red beads hurting at your throat
got anonymised in another town
I didn't go looking, wore dark glasses
To deepen reflection on pain

165

Endurance; just look at the dandelion
carrying the weight of the sun

166

A handbag's the Elysian mysteries
red lipstick bullets, my accessories

167

Fell downwards as a precursor to death
the bottom of the stairs a bloody pit

168

Everything's mythic by its own fiction
carry a story on the tongue
and expands into architecture

a morphic tide of possibilities
sometimes starts with a single word

169

Bad luck is on me, grief at life
in losing contact with the source
all those high heel pits on the mountain top

where inspiration sings
I gotta take it, fewer friends
go my way mine

170

Became for nothing, look I lost
my identity like a diamond ring

171

Her routed voice grew preconditioning
the likes of Sylvia Plath, Sexton,

brushed her teeth with honey to get it right
toothpaste is part of poetry

172

Chthonic go the underground
meet the right face in death
it's like the Circle line, strange attractor

173

Vines climbing upwards to the sun
juiced inspiration in their purple glow

174

I'm like the leader of the pack
a girl biker the one ahead
a doo-dah-run run doo-dah run

175

Left you behind, you never got it babe,
harmony, dance, fluent measure
like watching a single thought spin round

176

What's he to her, an accountable taste
met in a bar, his personality
like condom lube coating the truth

177

Nurture the garden, poetry the same,
red roses should lean shoulders together
like the meeting of two glasses of wine

178

Danger. I'm going mad madder
learning I'm toeing the edge of the edge

179

Wise, like honey in a jar
compounding flowers into a golden shine

180

Tonic pepped into gin botanicals
note each musicality on the tongue

181

Open emotion—giving this no take
on dyeing my intentions pink or blue

182

I gotta go even if going hurts
sometimes it's like walking into a door

183

Your bedroom massage, girl to girl
oblivion reaches a higher state
by ritual, each fingertip anoints oil

184

Can't walk across the river in red shoes
without projective telepathy

185

Those children's heroes always let them down
so too Dionysian orgiasts
drunk on unmanageable celebrity

186

Called you Adonis over and over
you one end of the sky me the other
and you sent Shelley as a virtual

187

Dawn, pink sky piling lavender on green
orange red a psychedelic poster
I pointed to with aqua fingernails

188

I heard her singing, a jeaned street busker
inviting me into her voice
and its variant subjectivities

189

Gold scatterings at dawn, like red sandals
open-toes, strappy show the ankle's curve

190

Arkheanassa
    ARKHEANASSA
name like I'm singing in a marble bath
or hearing an each come out the sky
walking to nowhere girl-spotting
making the dream into reality
by finding you to answer to that name

191

Half of my life behind my back
my drizzled hormones depleted
need a rejuvenating moisturiser

Q10 for oxidative stress.
Old age is a fly settled on the nose.
Take inspiration from her voice
and violet eyes island-hopping

itinerant poetry fills the clouds

192

Can't tell the voice from instrument
it's then you know it's coming through

193

I age beside you Gongyla
meaning youth grows brighter in memory
apples and acorns littering the ground
in bumpy September
    Sappho
you say, a name never grows old
it doesn't bruise on contact with the ground

194

The crowds converged on Ionia
a summer festival, folk-rock
coming and going on the wind
a dense crush surfed over by breezy riffs

and a child playing immersed in grasses
whatever occupies as game
find yourself you find the other

so Kallias reminded who is that
still scratching history

195

I

The moon's obscured, the Pleiades too.
Loneliness comes up in deep night
searching time hour by hour. I lie alone.

II

The moon's an opalescent fingernail
relative to my viewing point.
Can't see the Pleiades for dense cloud
nor all that glitter in red cosmic dust.

It's the red moon at equinox
freaks me scary. My pills don't work.
I'm lonely, curved into my bed
nights when the galaxies roar through my mind

like I'm better off dead

SNAKE DANCE

A SECOND VERSION
OF SAPPHO

1

Oh, Baby
The stunning hottie Aphrodite
outreach of a god's lightning orgasm
don't subjugate me to this sexy pull
I'll be the loser with a beat up heart

but heal me in my usual shattered mess
of dating all the wrong ones, girls who through
their own confusion leave me to crawl the floor,
break out of your father's mansion in the sky

be intuitive spontaneity
the sort of presence that arrives so fast
it overtakes the speed of light
like vision arrived reverse engineered

a torched-up vaporising flash.
You'll find me choked up in my room again,
distraught with loss, shampoo on the mirror,
demanding help. Girls break up girls like chairs.

You'll find me demented, distracted, mad,
she's gone, the only one, they always go,
leaving me writing poetry in blood,
and you won't change a thing, just look at me

and say most times the wrong comes right
and she'll return—I've heard it all before
they don't come back with the same nail polish
or shape a love bite into Prussian blue.

You're just my witness to the same old pain
irremediably there but stick around
as consolation I'll be up all night
knowing of course she won't be back again.

2

Out of Crete find me
standing naked in the trees
yellow apples popping
ooze, tangy libanum
offered as rite

in the crystal forest
where apples crash like yellow diamonds
and the water's cold
as shock

and roses see they're pouty red
throw conclusive shapes
like scented cloud shadows.
I want to sleep inside a rose
like Gertrude Stein.

Here horses stand in daisies
some of my girls sit under trees
stoned from an outdoors festival

white dresses green
from chlorophyll

I'm here with Kypris
pour wine into paper cups
amorous libation
instructing how we DANCE
DANCE DANCE

6

When you die it's terminal
there's no one cares beyond immediate grief
no share in Pierian roses
redder than those sold in Tesco.

Once you're lost in the departure hall
you'll join the homeless and invisible
sitting in doorways out of it
the dead don't know the dead because they're dead
don't own to names in the grey underworld

6 Variant

Dead, there won't be no recall
you're special, no red Pierian roses
to make an afternoon, no you,
only this virtual lined up with the dead
as though you faced a firing squad

7

At the ruined temple
Dika doing things with flowers
amazing marguerites
hair a trichological fetish
luxuriously sumptuous
she's making a crown
for the serendipitous muses
who kick in lyric

8

You'll come with spring Gongyla
bringing news of girls, girls predict
the first red-eyed narcissus

That messenger's entered my dreams again
the dodgy one, pathology
is it impending illness?

And if I long to die, it's that
there's a druggy lotus inside my dream
I'll only pick crossing the black river

8 Variant

This wait for spring Gongyla
it's a girl's thing extracting clothes
lighter than thought and it's our avatar

back with us, our predictive messenger
bringing worry, contact that puts
a twist in thinking clear

and death if it means crossing a river
has a lots as incentive
the smoke you're given on the other side

14

Idaos as messenger in the rain
greased Yamaha bike shouted—
'Hector and his muscled entourage
bring Andromache captive
(she's half-Asian/mixed ethnicity)
magenta eyes, size 2 feet,
she's got trunks of gold bracelets
a cache of coruscating jewels
like some Harrods ruined Saudi princess
picking diamonds like chocolates,'
sort of like that and the news broke

It was Hector's father mobilised
got the Illos gang out
into the hills
their women with them
noted for ankles
the size of diamond rings
and they danced crazily, raunchy, abandoned
to a guitar howling at the rainy sky
so fucking virtuoso that it bled

17

This teen runaway, she's so wild
I'm hexed under her black virulent spell
of Lydian street lore.
She's often in a plaid mini,
bare legs, don't know a hem
for sexiness surfs the ankle

17 Variant

Wild child, a leather jacket
suits you babe from the country
induces magic
without psychedelics.
Tough little bitch I'll teach ya yet
to wear a skirt the hem
resistant to the ankle

20

This guy he's got the look
stands your nipples out
breathes into your words his own
like two colours bleed a third.

He comes on even though you're not
one-on-one with men
puts me into stomping rage
burns by gut like green poison.

My mouth goes dry, can't see a thing,
my blood revs an arterial roar,
I'm drunk on gin, ouzo and beer,
I'd have him laid out on the floor.

My brain's explosive, you don't care
I'm beat up in a blender
don't know my shaking hands from feet
and if he touches you it's all over

20 Variant

That guy stands out, is he a god
time-slipped into our dimension,
he's all attention, listens out
your stories, summer on the beach.

He quickens though he knows you're gay,
it chokes me up you warm to him
my viscera tightening
third drink in, I can't look away.

I'm so jealous I'd smash the bar,
my tongue sticks to my mouth, can't see
for panicked recalcitrant daze
but hear your smoochy incredulity.

I sweat it through both hot and cold,
convulse at my expulsion from your life,
don't know the ceiling from the floor
I'm stood up, a third party go-between.

21

Clear out of the blue sky
a tutelary rush an avatar
sizzles nude in a red Phoenician shirt.

22

The word was out, she's out
Andromeda, the season's festivals
don't bring her back front of the stage
I read in graffiti SAPPHO
We love you oh
don't go
to Kypros for the one
with luminously violet eyes

she died a time, and now she's back again

24

Gongyla (such a sexy name)
come over here tonight and sing
chic aura that your looks create
leave me hoping to skin a dress
tubed on you like a ring

I don't pretend to worship paradigms
it's your sex makes me ache with need
the way you colour coloratura

24 Variant

I got it bad Gongyla la la
come over, sing to me with your guitar
la la it's your aura
and the hot number that you wear
la la such a sexy thing
can't separate the song from you
la la Gongyla

25

Anaktoria out of town
think back on mere member
use telepathy get
into me
I can hear
rappy metric of red high heels
see thunder in your lipsticked smile
moody mood break into me
sick of these Lydian terrorists
surveying us with weaponry

25 Variant

A puff of sea fog remember
back on me parallel timelines
telepathy our squirted frequency
luv you I can hear
heel-chatter of your walk
like cereal poured into a bowl
and your moodiness comes up
like an occluded cloud the police
hung out with riot shields and clubs

26

Mixing the hallucinogenic
magic in a jug
decanted to a bottle
Ermais doses the poison
the toxin comes up like an avatar,
you tip some outa new plant grows
with a psychoactive brain
we do it all together
for skyways vision
risen like an orange sun

26 Variant

Hallucinogenic mushrooms
we cook and jug the brew
hold out cups the psychedelic
brims in mixed with nectar
the god comes down into our collective
offer a libation
do it as community and spill some
to grow a hundred-headed flower

34

Atthis, I loved you honey,
time back when nothing happened
you locked the bedroom door,
didn't make up, address plain looks.

Now you hate the thought of me
hang two chandeliers in pierced ears
go chase a dike whose name ends in A
and goes nude except for earrings

34 Variant

Just ordinary Atthis—
and yet you knew the paradigm
NO MONEY NO HONEY
I didn't get a lick of your restraint
and now you got no time for me
go nosing our hot pheromones
of blonde A with a figure like a spoon

ANDROMEDA

40

A blush red apple, the one out of reach,
eludes the picker, acid shine,
it blazes there, the one they miss
intentionally, like seeing it's
subliminal, the breakage done
without snapping the spray.

The colour's like a mountain hyacinth
trodden flat to stain red
and deeper purple underfoot like a tattoo

43

SARDIS
how often she recalls our foggy shore
and me (Sappho) she'd have me sing
like I'd invented words

and danced like she was naked geometry.
Now she's that to Lydian dikes
unsurpassable as a loud red moon.

She dazzles, radiant personality
hangs out in fields thick with swathes of daisies
enhances shine in everything

roses scrolled like turbans, tangy clover,
and brings to mind Atthis runaway teen
in ripped jeans drove us all crazy

46

Mika, I'm cut up
you've taken Penthilea for your own
and grown cold on me
your voice is like crushed ice.
Sing to me, right down low,
a song on my porch, need it now
right bottom blues

46 Variant

Mika you've slit my throat
run off with blonde Penthilea
taken a villa (note two A's
rhyme like maracas)
so make me a song each phrase
sung slowly Iowa blues
for impending evening

54

Arkheanassa and Gorgo
(names that sound like edible flowers)
sleep together, girls married
to girls as triangular fit
and Pleistodike (name like a tropical
lily's vulva)
was sometime between Gongyla and Gorgo
like avocado as a sandwich filler

54 Variant

Pleistodike's the instigator
of threesomes with A and G
(say the three names you get a syllabic
sponge cake) wears two black eye-strikes
as differentiated cult, rides a bike
between beaches, loves Gongyla and Gorgo
paints their toenails black, writes SAME SEX
on each ass, S like a snake

56

Obsidian
ophidian
a girlie vivarium
Muses come down again
in strapless gold sandals
at my invocation

57

Search your guitar
the bride's dressed in purple
your voice opens like a flower
in this gay configuration
the snaky one's got size 3 feet
you could fit in a spoon
dipped into honey

67

Pollyanna and
Polyanaktidas
(polysyllabic mantras)
gone on the hazy ferry
I loved them like downmooded blues
Middling in topaz

67 Variant

Pollyanna/
Polyanaktides
gone without goodbye
compounded into a poem
no bigger than a thumbnail
painted aqua like the sky

67 Variant

I lick Polyanktidas
    to multiples
sensitised by a vibrator
    the music in our heads
it was mine someone else's
    in this sticky lubricity
where sex seems
    oracular
an orgy's an orgiastic convention
    of body-hopping
without names
    as volcanic signature

75

This girl gang celebrate you all night long
as lucky, as her chosen one.
She'll wear a violet dress for you
size 10 that's tighter than her skin.

Go get your boy gang together
to drink all night, make noise.
Up on the roof you'll hear a biker burn
towards the house, a Harley courier

75 Variant

They're at your door Mister
girl aggro, but they sing to you
about how the only divide
she has from you's a violet dress
you can't tell from the light

or closer

82

May she find you Cypris
severe as colliding with a door
and as for Doricha who sold sex
(real name Lolita)
still unrequited she'll be onto you
offering to even strip her skin

82 Variant

Doncha go for Cypris hun
she's cold shower austere
(read in the footnotes she's from Naucratis)
Dorichaher tongue's like jelly
she's looking for you in the bath-house
where your figure's cloned by steam

87

I've a girl whose orange hair
reminds me of a marigold
Kleis is her name
Our grammar's tongue to tongue
Hotter than Lydia's, she's what
I've waited for hung up

on choosing her a bandana
as a sign of our cult
as outlaws on the coast

88

Inspiration Eros
arrives like a purple lightning flash
cooks my neural circuitry
hurts all over after

93

Curls
brush
gold lyre
blonde
better
than fingers

93 Variant

She plays
it with her hair
on strings
not fingers

76

Nine is the number made me happy
poetry lexical mantra
my way brought envy, it's ahead
being read in another century

76 Variant

Started young, words bouncing in
demanding melody
couldn't separate from what it did
POETRY
numinously luminous

and now the girls upfront
we walk to a wedding on the road
can't take my eyes off you and you
they say we'll find the mountain
where my inspiration glows

CODA

They said if the future's complete
Leonard Cohen went before me
carrying a guitar like a coffin
with my girls up the mountain

78

Bitterer than Americano
her leaving. All that terror in my heart
her last squeeze on the patio
trying to wish the best for each other

like watching a ship on the horizon
nudge our past. I loved her that bad
I'd put red braids in her hair
stick a rose above her ear
oil her body languorously

pile up red cushions
under her blonde spill, but she's gone

78 Variant

Reactivated my death wish
the terror of her gone, hysteria
like a jammed car horn, colour squeezed
out of my life to monochrome
and her knotted equivocation
before screaming my name and gone
braids in her hair, one thrown look back
slicing my heart like an orange

82

May she find you Cypris
severe as colliding with a door
and as for Doricha who sold sex
(real name Lolita)
still unrequited she'll be onto you
offering to even strip her skin

82 Variant

Doncha go for Cypris hun
she's cold shower austere
(read in the footnotes she's from Naucratis)
Dorichaher tongue's like jelly
she's looking for you in the bath-house
where your figure's cloned by steam

87

I've a girl whose orange hair
reminds me of a marigold
Kleis is her name
our grammar's tongue on tongue
hotter than Lydia's, she's what
I've waited for hung up

on choosing her a bandana
as sign of our cult
as proscribed outlaws on the coast

87 Variant

Her hair's dosed with henna
sort of marigold oomph.
She's Kleis, new acquisition
to my sosorial promiscuity
better than Lydia
I love her so it hurts

and kit her with a bandana
I knot at the back of her head
like joining two spaghetti strands

88

Inspiration Eros
arrives like a purple lightning flash
cooks my neural circuitry
hurts all over after

96

This teen called Leda wading through high grass
faced down a purple egg near lavender
her suede boots slaughtered by the damp
knew she'd interacted with a genie

119

A red Phrygian carpet
woven by a sex-slave
(they keep a stable round the coast)
she's yours or mine
her yellow shirt
red dress (clash)
hair accessories
(Japanese do it best)
mostly it's the red carpet
gives her vermilion soles
if you imagine them lifting

119 Variant

Yellow shirt in a traffic haze
red dress (a hand-me-down)
she's mine sometimes
yours what's it matter
pretty eyes violet
(prefer that to blue)
got her hair up
her red Phrygian carpet
rolled out when she's dead
to cross one side to the other

123

Black virulent dreams
oeneric smoke burnt offerings
like a gutted car
the place is hexed no hope
get out go back to games
in the Jacuzzi where steam
is an orgasmic G

124

No one like her under the sun
I see so many on the beach
Preening selfies she means
LONELINESS attracts no one
when you're that alienated

124 Variant

She's a legend can't help it
a mocha sun-worshipper
her intelligence like radio signal
from a roaming extraterrestrial
none like her on quartzy pink beach
sitting solitary where surf collapses

135

The Muses hang out in Pieria
topless in violet haze. When they bite me
I'm whipped violently by luxurious hair

143

Seven ways of terror 7
the house in the laurel tree's empty
I hid poems with a mouse there
seven not six seven
and you babe imperturbably serene
came with your mouth full of kisses
open arms counting to seven

145

You too, Kalliopa,
be yourself so much you
you speak poetry as ordinary

146

I called you
filled your mouth with girls
love songs cut by my harp
designer clothes I called you
older now hair dyed black
as a cellar bar
still squeezing poems from the rose-pink dawn
called you minus cells
disappeared from my body
oxidisation of the brain
called you wanting more
love than a lover gives
or receives my window on a pink sky
rehabilitating youth I called you
but not with my mouth

167

Me away from them
poetry rolls like thunder through my veins
it's an inspirational sauna
slapping me mad
Andromeda

and you Tyndarides
your property portfolio
(rams palaces like gold fillings
into real estate)

your security detail
like military thugs
rock muscle on the door

167 Variant

It's hot in me incantation
inspirational juice
like wrestling with shapes
slippery as shampoo
ANDROMEDA

Poets get no money
and you Tyndarides
buy top-end palaces
money laundering a river
from an offshore barrio

you're surrounded by minders
marshals, muscled guards,
poetry's richer than light
in its amazing photonic pour

175

Barbitos. Baromas. Barmos—
black-hooded desperados
names like a pharma brand
sedative hypnotic
who were they to us?

212

The youngest on our luscious summer break
all that green tangled quiet
under trees, games she played in Ionia
repeated to our city cult
toplessly colonising a meadow
so clear you'd see each atom in position

212 Variant

Memory always treats summer
on the run on orange beaches
or backed up by country quiet
naming flowers like they do in Ionia
as a botanical canto

and we go back later as urban
rehabilitation loose in grasses
Kallias they called her
the one who walked there blindfold

213

Moon and the Pleiades down
on my orbital curve
midnight behind me now the desperate hours
I lie alone

213 Variant

I'm fetched up solitary, no moon
or stars, just a smoggy halo
after midnight, embracing a pillow
because she's gone

213 Variant

Alone, searching for my sex toy,
moon and stars smudged out by our atmosphere
it's lonely 3 a.m. then 4
she's gone I know it back to him

A PARTIAL LIST OF SNUGGLY BOOKS

G. ALBERT AURIER *Elsewhere and Other Stories*
S. HENRY BERTHOUD *Misanthropic Tales*
LÉON BLOY *The Desperate Man*
LÉON BLOY *The Tarantulas' Parlor and Other Unkind Tales*
ÉLÉMIR BOURGES *The Twilight of the Gods*
JAMES CHAMPAGNE *Harlem Smoke*
FÉLICIEN CHAMPSAUR *The Latin Orgy*
FÉLICIEN CHAMPSAUR
  The Emerald Princess and Other Decadent Fantasies
BRENDAN CONNELL *Clark*
BRENDAN CONNELL *Unofficial History of Pi Wei*
RAFAELA CONTRERAS *The Turquoise Ring and Other Stories*
ADOLFO COUVE *When I Think of My Missing Head*
QUENTIN S. CRISP *Aiaigasa*
QUENTIN S. CRISP *Graves*
LADY DILKE *The Outcast Spirit and Other Stories*
CATHERINE DOUSTEYSSIER-KHOZE *The Beauty of the Death Cap*
ÉDOUARD DUJARDIN *Hauntings*
BERIT ELLINGSEN *Now We Can See the Moon*
BERIT ELLINGSEN *Vessel and Solsvart*
ENRIQUE GÓMEZ CARRILLO *Sentimental Stories*
EDMOND AND JULES DE GONCOURT *Manette Salomon*
REMY DE GOURMONT *From a Faraway Land*
GUIDO GOZZANO *Alcina and Other Stories*
EDWARD HERON-ALLEN *The Complete Shorter Fiction*
RHYS HUGHES *Cloud Farming in Wales*
J.-K. HUYSMANS *Knapsacks*
COLIN INSOLE *Valerie and Other Stories*
JUSTIN ISIS *Pleasant Tales II*
JUSTIN ISIS (editor) *Marked to Die: A Tribute to Mark Samuels*
JUSTIN ISIS AND DANIEL CORRICK (editors)
  Drowning in Beauty: The Neo-Decadent Anthology

VICTOR JOLY *The Unknown Collaborator and Other Legendary Tales*
MARIE KRYSINSKA *The Path of Amour*
BERNARD LAZARE *The Mirror of Legends*
BERNARD LAZARE *The Torch-Bearers*
MAURICE LEVEL *The Shadow*
JEAN LORRAIN *Errant Vice*
JEAN LORRAIN *Fards and Poisons*
JEAN LORRAIN *Masks in the Tapestry*
JEAN LORRAIN *Monsieur de Bougrelon and Other Stories*
JEAN LORRAIN *Nightmares of an Ether-Drinker*
JEAN LORRAIN *The Soul-Drinker and Other Decadent Fantasies*
ARTHUR MACHEN *N*
ARTHUR MACHEN *Ornaments in Jade*
CAMILLE MAUCLAIR *The Frail Soul and Other Stories*
CATULLE MENDÈS *Bluebirds*
CATULLE MENDÈS *For Reading in the Bath*
CATULLE MENDÈS *Mephistophela*
ÉPHRAÏM MIKHAËL *Halyartes and Other Poems in Prose*
LUIS DE MIRANDA *Who Killed the Poet?*
OCTAVE MIRBEAU *The Death of Balzac*
CHARLES MORICE *Babels, Balloons and Innocent Eyes*
DAMIAN MURPHY *Daughters of Apostasy*
DAMIAN MURPHY *The Star of Gnosia*
KRISTINE ONG MUSLIM *Butterfly Dream*
PHILOTHÉE O'NEDDY *The Enchanted Ring*
YARROW PAISLEY *Mendicant City*
URSULA PFLUG *Down From*
ADOLPHE RETTÉ *Misty Thule*
JEAN RICHEPIN *The Bull-Man and the Grasshopper*
DAVID RIX *A Blast of Hunters*
DAVID RIX *A Suite in Four Windows*
FREDERICK ROLFE (Baron Corvo) *Amico di Sandro*
FREDERICK ROLFE (Baron Corvo)
   An Ossuary of the North Lagoon and Other Stories

JASON ROLFE *An Archive of Human Nonsense*
BRIAN STABLEFORD (editor)
   Decadence and Symbolism: A Showcase Anthology
BRIAN STABLEFORD (editor) *The Snuggly Satyricon*
BRIAN STABLEFORD *The Insubstantial Pageant*
BRIAN STABLEFORD *Spirits of the Vasty Deep*
BRIAN STABLEFORD *The Truths of Darkness*
COUNT ERIC STENBOCK *Love, Sleep & Dreams*
COUNT ERIC STENBOCK *Myrtle, Rue & Cypress*
COUNT ERIC STENBOCK *The Shadow of Death*
COUNT ERIC STENBOCK *Studies of Death*
MONTAGUE SUMMERS *The Bride of Christ and Other Fictions*
MONTAGUE SUMMERS *Six Ghost Stories*
GILBERT-AUGUSTIN THIERRY *The Blonde Tress and The Mask*
GILBERT-AUGUSTIN THIERRY *Reincarnation and Redemption*
DOUGLAS THOMPSON *The Fallen West*
TOADHOUSE *Gone Fishing with Samy Rosenstock*
TOADHOUSE *Living and Dying in a Mind Field*
RUGGERO VASARI *Raun*
JANE DE LA VAUDÈRE *The Demi-Sexes and The Androgynes*
JANE DE LA VAUDÈRE *The Double Star and Other Occult Fantasies*
JANE DE LA VAUDÈRE *The Mystery of Kama and Brahma's Courtesans*
JANE DE LA VAUDÈRE *The Priestesses of Mylitta*
JANE DE LA VAUDÈRE *Syta's Harem and Pharaoh's Lover*
JANE DE LA VAUDÈRE *Three Flowers and The King of Siam's Amazon*
JANE DE LA VAUDÈRE *The Witch of Ecbatana and The Virgin of Israel*
AUGUSTE VILLIERS DE L'ISLE-ADAM *Isis*
RENÉE VIVIEN AND HÉLÈNE DE ZUYLEN DE NYEVELT
   Faustina and Other Stories
RENÉE VIVIEN *Lilith's Legacy*
RENÉE VIVIEN *A Woman Appeared to Me*
TERESA WILMS MONTT *In the Stillness of Marble*
TERESA WILMS MONTT *Sentimental Doubts*
KAREL VAN DE WOESTIJNE *The Dying Peasant*

www.ingramcontent.com/pod-product-compliance
Lightning Source LLC
Chambersburg PA
CBHW031100080526
44587CB00011B/762